In the Stillness

journal belongs to...

© 2017 Ranch House Press
All rights reserved. Printed in the United States of America.

www.annettebridges.com

ISBN: 978-1-946371-22-5

Journal Prompts

In the Stillness

1. Write a prayer on behalf of a loved one. Thank God for them and describe your thoughts about this person to God.
2. Take a prayer walk outside and for everything you see, give thanks.
3. List out your priorities or decisions you must make in the next week. Give them to God and ask him to lead you every step of the way.
4. Copy the Lord's Prayer from Matthew 6:9-13. Then rewrite the prayer using your own words.
5. Father, show me …
6. I pray that I am able to …
7. Father, give me the courage to …
8. In moments when I am afraid …
9. I find I feel God's presence most when …
10. Verses/passages that give you hope
11. Verses/passages to pray when your heart is broken
12. Verses/passages to pray when you need to forgive
13. Verses/passages to pray when waiting is hard
14. Verses/passages to pray when you don't know what to do
15. Verses/passages to pray when you're ill
16. Write a prayer for when you don't know what or how to pray
17. I have been driven many times upon my knees by the overwhelming conviction that I had nowhere else to go. My own wisdom and that of all about me seemed insufficient for that day. ~ Abraham Lincoln
18. When life gives you more than you can stand, kneel.
19. Prayer is when you talk to God, meditation is when God talks to you.
20. If you have time to worry, you have time to pray.
21. Prayer is not asking. It is a longing of the soul. It is a daily admission of one's weakness. ~ Gandhi
22. The word LISTEN contains the same letters as the word SILENT.
23. Be still. The quieter you become, the more you can hear. ~ Ram Dass
24. In the midst of movement and chaos, keep stillness inside of you. ~ Deepak Chopra
25. So the darkness shall be the light, and the stillness the dancing. ~ T.S. Eliot
26. Listen in silence because if your heart is full of other things you cannot hear the voice of God. ~ Mother Teresa
27. Quiet the mind and the soul will speak. ~ Ma Jaya Sati Bhagavati
28. When you lose touch with your inner stillness, you lose touch with yourself. When you lose touch with yourself, you lose yourself in the world. ~ Eckhart Tolle
29. Within yourself is a stillness, a sanctuary to which you can retreat at any time and be yourself. ~ Herman Hess
30. Peace. It does not mean to be in a place where there is no noise, trouble or hard work. It means to be in the midst of those things and still be calm in your heart.
31. Stillness. Noun. 1. Silence; quiet; hush. 2. The absence of motion.

color your world

ABOUT the CREATOR

Annette Bridges is an author, publisher and women's retreat host on a mission to help every woman realize her story is extraordinary, valuable and noteworthy.

She has published the *Color Your World Journal Series* and formed a journal club to provide community, support and tools for women to record their ideas, feelings, experiences, memories and all the important details of their lives.

Before writing books and publishing journals and coloring books, this former public school and homeschool educator spent a decade writing hundreds of helpful, instructive, and light-hearted columns published by Texas newspapers, parenting magazines, websites and bloggers.

Annette lives on a Texas cattle ranch with her husband John, dachshund Lady and lots of cows. She can drive a tractor but only if wearing a fresh coat of lipstick and it's not her pedicure day!

You can learn more about Annette's books and products, blogs and videos as well as her women's retreats and other events at www.annettebridges.com.

Look for her on social media, too!

MESSAGE from the PUBLISHER

The *Color Your World Journal Series* is a pathway to self-discovery. It's where you write notes to yourself. Be your own cheerleader. Give yourself encouragement. Tell yourself what you're grateful for. Celebrate you!

There are countless reasons to keep a journal including collecting favorite recipes, listing goals and celebrating every experience and every one that's near and dear to you. A journal provides a home for the memories and lessons learned that you never want to forget.

Why a niche journal?

If you're anything like me, you have a journal (or even two or three journals) where you write anything and everything about anything and everything. My challenge comes when trying to find something I've written. I flip and flip through the pages of my two, three or four journals trying to find whatever it is. I never remember which journal I wrote down my whatever's!!

The solution? A niche journal! A journal that has a specific focus and theme! A journal where you can record your ideas, inspirations and things you want to remember in the appropriate journal.

Why big unlined paper?

Because big unlined paper is needed to record big ideas, dreams and memories! You need room to grow, stretch and expand. You need space to think beyond the confines of what you've always done, to pursue new dreams, discover your power and reimagine your purpose again and again. You need pages without lines and limitations to reconnect with your creative, perfectly imperfect self.

Plus, big unlined paper gives you space for more than words. You have plenty of room to doodle, draw or post photographs and clippings, too.

Why color is important?

When you journal, use colored pens and markers! Your world doesn't happen in black and white. Your life should be lived and written about in many colors. Even dark and sad memories feel lighter and brighter when told in color.

Journaling in color affects your mood and perception of your world. Colors evoke calm, cheer and comfort. Using color can lift your spirit and inspire your imagination. You may be surprised by all the beautiful benefits from adding more color into your life story.

When journaling, give yourself time to listen to your heart and reflect. Breathe in the moments. Feel. Be quiet. Let yourself be totally and thoroughly present with your thoughts. Let your heart transform you and teach you new insights. Open your mind to consider new ideas and possibilities. You may find that what your heart teaches will be life changing.

www.ingramcontent.com/pod-product-compliance
Lightning Source LLC
Chambersburg PA
CBHW051252110526
44588CB00025B/2971